# THE BOOK OF UNCOMMON HOURS

a book of haiku poetry

# Other Books by Rachel

**Poetry**
*This is How You Know*
*Life: a definition of terms*

**Essay**
*Parenthood: Has Anyone Seen My Sanity?*
*The Life-Changing Madness of Tidying Up After Children*
*This Life With Boys*
*We Count it All Joy: Essays*

**To see all the books Rachel has written, please click or visit the link below:**
www.racheltoalson.com/writing

RACHEL TOALSON

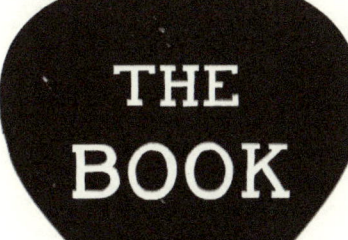

THE
BOOK

OF
UNCOMMON
HOURS

a book of haiku poetry

BATLEE
PRESS

Batlee Press
PO Box 591596
San Antonio, TX 78259

Copyright ©2018 by Rachel Toalson
All rights reserved.

No part of this book may be reproduced or transmitted in any form or by any means, electronic or mechanical, including photocopying and recording, or by any information storage and retrieval system, without permission in writing. For information, address Batlee Press, PO Box 591596, San Antonio, TX 78259.

The author appreciates your taking the time to read her work. Please consider leaving a review wherever you bought it, or telling your friends how much you enjoyed it. Both of those help get the book into the hands of new readers, which is incredibly important for authors. Thank you for your support.
www.racheltoalson.com

Manufactured in the United States of America

First Edition—2018/Cover designed by Toalson Marketing
www.toalsonmarketing.com

*To my boys—*
*You turn my common world into an uncommon masterpiece*

# Introduction

It is astonishingly easy to get captured and locked away in the drudgery of a day—wake, eat, work, eat, sleep, and do it all again. It seems so unremarkable, these days that, collectively, pass faster than we can fathom.

But the moments—these are the places where the remarkable exist.

In one of my recent funks (and there are many), I decided to try an experiment: find beauty in the moments of my day—the wonderful ones, but also (and especially) the hard ones. I decided to take a slice of my day and examine these seemingly common yet uncommon moments.

I captured the essence of these moments—these hours, if you will—into haiku poetry, because it takes only a moment to jot down seventeen syllables (though much longer to revise and perfect). In these pages, you will see how quickly a moment can turn from bad to good, the way a mind can jump from worry to wonder and back again, what it's like to live in the spaces of the common hours that become uncommon in our notice.

I will take you from the hour I wake up—a little after 4 a.m.—to the hour I fall asleep—a little after 9 p.m. I will show you anxiety, frustration, and fear, but I will also show you joy and love and hope. I will show you life.

These are the uncommon hours. Let's live them well.

4:00 AM

**4:15:00**

The alarm lifts me
from sleep with a sweet, gentle
melody. I wake.

**4:15:01**

In this stage of life
I wake up every morning
with a deep headache.

**4:15:02**

The to-do list is
never done when you work for
yourself and have kids.

**4:15:03**

Money worries keep
coming back—will ever this
lean season be done?

**4:15:07**

Get up and face a
brand new day, a brand new slate.
Isn't it lovely?

## 4:15:49
The early morning
hours, when the house sleeps still—
these are life-giving.

## 4:16:00
At times, alone can
be a breath of fresh air—when
one is a parent.

## 4:17:02
The scratch of a pen
against paper is one of
my favorite sounds.

## 4:43:56
Sometimes, when I wait
for my world to wake, I pen
a poem of love.

## 4:43:57
Sometimes I pen my
thoughts—what happened yesterday,
what's coming today.

## 4:43:58

Sometimes I pen
randomness: thoughts, wonderings,
the questions of real life.

## 4:43:59

At times they are
philosophical, sounding something
like what follows:

## 4:45:30

If we are who we
believe we are, then we must
believe in greatness.

## 4:45:32

The only journey
we really make is the one
that happens within.

## 4:45:34

We are always
enough for the world we have been
given. This is truth.

## 4:46:23

Insects hum all around,
hanging on to summer—
fall lifts the edges.

## 4:47:29

I'm gone before they're
up, to run and think and breathe
in a still morning.

## 4:51:17

Wind whistles across
the canyon this morning, like
it's telling secrets.

**5:01:07**

A low humming in
the distance confirms the world
has now awakened.

**5:04:18**

The wind whistles down
the canyon and I feel it
shaking inside me.

**5:04:20**

The philosophical
wanderings continue
as I greet my day.

**5:04:23**

What do we have to
offer the world but the
splendid whole of ourselves?

**5:06:37**

Life is both a dream
and a fear, and it never
can be understood.

## 5:17:21

The wind rustles through
my hair even though I'm walking:
promising fall.

## 5:18:01

Back home, he has a
mug of green tea waiting for
me. It hastens love.

## 5:19:41

Sometimes the love is
so wide, large I feel like my
heart can only burst.

## 5:21:24

A breeze, reaching through
the window, whispers of hope:
It's a brand new day.

## 5:27:52

The moment unfolds
quietly, ushers in
profound awakening.

## 5:47:46

Coffee drips in the
next room. I'm still in silence,
breathing in my day.

## 5:58:02

The patter of their
footsteps before the sun's up
gives me grave nightmares.

## 5:58:11

I get up early
in the morning so kids can
steal my quiet time.

## 5:58:16

This is a morning
when all they seem to do is
whine, and me with them.

## 5:59:59

I greet every day
with surging hope and a
persistent exhaustion.

6:00 AM

## 6:02:12

The sky unfolds gray
and heavy, wind gentle, sun
peering through the fog.

## 6:02:26

"I had this weird dream"
is the first thing they say to
me every morning.

## 6:02:37

It quickly devolves—
I can't do something they want
and the world's ending.

## 6:02:45

Whining, complaining—
they all give me a headache,
so go back to bed.

## 6:02:46

(I feel like there is
a theme this morning: it's a
morning fit to whine.)

## 6:02:47

(No thank you. No thank
you. No thank you, no thank you
no thank you. No thanks.)

## 6:03:59

They won't go back to
bed—frankly, my dear, I'm too
tired to give a damn.

## 6:05:01

Peppermint green tea
is my morning coffee—I'm
useless without it.

## 6:07:16

Sign papers, prepare
breakfast, put it on the table
before wake time.

## 6:29:34

The world will unfold
according to the lens through
which we filter it.

## 6:29:35

I adjust mine: there,
now I can see the beauty
of this wondrous life.

## 6:30:00

The house is stirring.
Some of them still sleep. I wake
them with a soft song.

## 6:30:04

Their voices drift in
from the library, soft, sweet
childlike. Listen.

## 6:30:37

My least favorite
thing is when they wake up with
whining on their mind.

## 6:30:38

It's barely morning
and already they are driving
me so crazy.

## 6:30:39
(Their whining makes me
want to whine—and sometimes I
play the game with them.)

## 6:33:57
They dress up in clothes
that don't match; they don't know the
rules—I hope it lasts.

## 6:34:22
The back door stands
open. The air is crisp today,
feeling like new starts.

## 6:34:24
(Someone's gone out to
look for his missing shoes—same
drill every morning.)

## 6:34:31
I don't even tell
them to close the door, so lovely
does the breeze feel.

## 6:35:04

A gentle hum of
voices—singing, talking, the
symphony of life.

## 6:36:46

A washer shakes in
the background. Silverware scrapes.
Boys mumble. Morning.

## 6:37:12

They talk so much
about anything at all and
don't try to make sense.

## 6:38:20

As soon as they sit
down they start complaining about
what's for breakfast.

## 6:38:21

"I don't like this," they
say. "Not surprised," I say. The
story of mornings.

## 6:38:22
The ungratefulness
of children is most fervent
in the morning.

## 6:57:36
The sky's now looking
eerie—a yellow-gray,
worrisome to one son.

## 6:57:37
It's no longer cool;
a hot breath gusts through the door,
disappointing us.

## 6:57:38
(September is the
dumbest month in Texas—should
be cool, but it's not.)

## 6:57:39
(September is, too,
the month when my mom was born—
so not the dumbest.)

## 6:58:47

No, you cannot take
the extra phone to school; it's
right down the road. Safe.

## 6:58:48

Temper raging, he
storms about the house, aiming
his hand at a door.

## 6:58:49

(He doesn't realize
his reaction tells me there's
more to it than safe.)

## 6:58:50

(Kids think their parents
don't know what they want—when we
nearly always do.)

## 6:59:31

They're silly, then they're
serious in the same breath.
Don't know when to laugh.

## 6:59:59

I am always in
a hurry—could this mean my
life's too big for me?

**7:10:04**

The clouds are heavy
now, gray puffs low in the sky.
Humidity soars.

**7:11:14**

A mist hovers on
the green, wetting our hair as
we're walking to school.

**7:12:58**

The sound of whine is
like a blue whale obliterating
my last nerve.

**7:12:59**

(He's whining about
his shoes, which he says are too
loose on his right foot.)

**7:13:01**

(He's whining about
how he never gets to ride
his scooter to school.)

**7:13:04**
(He's whining about
how he didn't win the foot
race with his brothers.)

**7:13:18**
Supermom today
looks like leaving half of them
behind for the walk.

**7:14:02**
Expectations are
the most common cause of
crippling disappointment.

**7:15:34**
For a moment, the
sun breaks through the clouds, like a
welcoming embrace.

**7:15:35**
The sun burns my cheek.
Wind puffs my hair, tickling my
nose, promising fall.

## 7:34:01

They pass out flowers
that bring a smile to every
person's morning face.

## 7:34:29

When there are no flowers
they pick wild grass to
give all who pass them.

## 7:42:41

The house seems quiet:
today is a school day and
half of them are gone.

## 7:45:16

Now it's time to clear
away the breakfast mess—did
animals eat here?

## 7:45:21

Back and forth between
sink and table; they forgot
to rinse out their bowls.

## 7:45:22
Teaching boys to clean
up after themselves is a
never-ending job.

## 7:45:37
Women have been called
queens—but who would want to rule
their mundane kingdom?

## 7:45:59
I have a little
companion who follows me
wherever I go.

## 7:46:04
This kingdom in which
I am queen is a lovely
one; I'd sure take it.

## 7:47:00
It's the coolest morning
it's been all season and
they won't go outside.

## 7:47:26

They're pushing each other
on a wheeled toy—but the
baby pushes most.

## 7:51:11

Clinks, clanks, pellets clicking—
they play make believe and
bring me along, too.

## 7:51:15

He holes under a
pillow, imagining the
darkest world of space.

## 7:52:46

He brings me a square,
tries to tell me what it is
in baby language.

## 7:52:47

I listen like I
understand; he spins a long,
elaborate tale.

## 7:54:28

Every morning he
sits on my lap for stories
and I smell his hair.

## 7:59:08

He races to get
another book; reading time
is never finished.

## 7:59:11

He stretches out on
the arm of my chair, wiggling,
giggling, and reading.

## 7:59:13

They are robed in song
this morning, so we go about
the day smiling.

8:00 AM

## 8:00:00

It's only eight o'clock
and already they are
fighting each other.

## 8:01:56

I need to make a
phone call—it's a terrifying
prospect for me.

## 8:01:59

But it must be done;
someone's asking for something
and I must answer.

## 8:02:00

I must answer no;
it's the only answer I
can possibly give.

## 8:02:13

No is the hardest
answer to give when people
really want your time.

## 8:02:18

The biggest mistakes
in my life happened when I
said yes but meant no.

## 8:02:23

The question is
repeated: I answer no, as
I had planned to do.

## 8:02:34

"No" is a gift of
freedom sometimes—now my time
is my family's.

## 8:07:03

Five minutes of not
paying attention and they're
tearing up the house.

## 8:07:12

Two minutes after
they sit down with a toy they're
done. It's exhausting.

## 8:07:15
If they would listen
to instructions, life would be
easier for them.

## 8:07:16
If they would listen
to instructions, life would be
easier for me.

## 8:07:17
This is not the way
a mother is supposed to
think; but she does, still.

## 8:07:22
It's okay; I'm not
a bad mom for acknowledging
that twins are hard.

## 8:07:23
They *are* hard; that doesn't
change my love for them—it
is fierce, motherly.

## 8:07:24

What would we do if
we had no masks? Tell the truth?
Live in glass houses?

## 8:07:25

I'd rather tell the
truth than live in a prison
of my own making.

## 8:14:02

They're already hungry
again, asking for a
snack—when is lunchtime?

## 8:14:12

The bananas are
green—they'll be eaten before
they even get spots.

## 8:28:10

He follows me through
the house, talking of wonderful
things all the way.

## 8:35:14

Clothes tumble dry low,
children roar, music thumps—just
a regular day.

## 8:43:50

Reading poetry
compels me to take a good
long look at myself.

## 8:43:51

Yesterday I yelled
at the two who have a hard
time choosing what's best.

## 8:43:54

Yesterday I didn't
spend as much time with them
as I needed to.

## 8:43:57

Yesterday I ate
two brownies and three chocolate
peppermint patties.

## 8:43:58
(They were small treats, but
not small failures on the healthy
living spectrum.)

## 8:43:59
It's hard not to
regret, so I choose to live now,
free of yesterday.

## 8:44:01
I look at my children,
who do this so well—what
can I learn from them?

## 8:44:03
They sing, they dance, they
talk without inhibition.
Kids live life fully.

## 8:44:04
I want to be that
kind of great: sing, dance, talk
without inhibition.

## 8:52:12

They bring me letters:
A, then B, then M, curious
about the sounds.

## 8:53:21

A plastic crocodile,
a rock in its mouth, blue
eyes dancing in mirth.

## 8:53:32

His laughter is one
of the greatest sounds bullying
the silences.

## 8:56:11

Listening to the
quiet makes me thankful there
are LEGOs and books.

## 8:57:03

The sound of LEGOs
clash and snap as they build, dream,
imagine new worlds.

## 8:58:45

Little boy is reading
to his brothers—it's the
sweetest thing ever.

## 8:58:53

Sometimes the best way
to say "I am here" is to
sit and stay a while.

9:00 AM

**9:02:12**

He gives a play by
play for everything he does.
Tiring. Endearing.

**9:02:13**

Sometimes when they talk
my mind runs away with a
thought—untamable.

**9:05:16**

His tuneless melody
reaches me in the kitchen.
I start to sing.

**9:11:32**

He's playing with blocks
quiet as can be—the last
one, the easiest.

**9:13:43**

He keeps bringing me
pieces of dirt and mud, as
if I'm his keeper.

## 9:13:44

I'll be his keeper
as long as he'll let me—I
know it won't be long.

## 9:13:45

All children must grow
up; all parents must resist
the urge to keep them.

## 9:13:46

He is my last baby—
so I pocket all the
pieces of dirt, mud,

## 9:13:47

as if it, too, will
somehow be preserved forever
in memory.

## 9:13:48

Time slips by on
silent wings, and there's nothing I
can do to slow it.

## 9:13:49

I kiss the top of
his head, breathe in his still-
baby scent—mine for now.

## 9:13:50

I don't want to escape
life—I simply don't want
it to escape me.

## 9:22:11

They run outside to
play, bored with the blocks they've been
using to build planes.

## 9:22:12

I follow them, like
a shadow; I love to hear
them play, dream, and laugh.

## 9:22:13

It's suffocating
when you step outside—humidity's
relentless.

## 9:31:47

I sort through papers,
see one I'll have to keep—late
homework assignment.

## 9:31:48

One son hasn't been
turning work in; school's too
easy for him to try.

## 9:31:49

What good's intelligence
if you don't have ambition
to use it well?

## 9:31:50

I try not to pressure
them, but I know the gift
of education.

## 9:31:51

How do you transfer
that knowing to a child who
grows up in privilege?

**9:31:52**

They are not their grades,
but expectations exist:
he can do better.

**9:31:53**

I don't care if he's
the best; I only want him
to try his own best.

**9:31:54**

I file away
the talk for later, slip the
paper in a stack.

**9:39:23**

"Mama, will you read
to us?" they ask, and the answer
is always, *Yes*.

**9:39:35**

They shove three stories
toward me, climb into my
lap, one on each knee.

## 9:45:58

We read and read and
read and not once do I grow
weary of reading.

## 9:46:10

We're finally finished,
no more books to read right now.
I jot down some notes.

## 9:47:17

If you're low on good
ideas, all you really
need to do is read.

## 9:48:00

They are lost in a
moment of shared mirth; I pick
up my pen to write.

## 9:48:01

Writing preserves a
moment, brings my attention
fully into now.

## 9:48:09

Little boy wants to
play catch with me, so I put
down my pen and play.

## 9:54:55

I turn my back for
one minute and he's destroying
a camera stand.

## 9:54:56

Anger flashes hot
and wild; how many times have
we told him hands off?

## 9:54:57

It's amazing how
fast a morning can crumble.
I stop, repair, try.

## 9:55:00

The forgiveness of
children is both astounding
and sweetly humbling.

10:00 AM

**10:00:01**
They race outside to
climb on swings, jump on the
trampoline, and giggle.

**10:00:59**
They are jumping from
swings, trying to see who flies
highest. Daring boys.

**10:01:34**
Lightning forks through the
sky; I call them back in to
their disappointment.

**10:01:48**
*I missed you*, he says.
in his toddler voice, and my
heart swells full inside.

**10:03:02**
The sky has drawn its
gray curtain. It hangs near the
ground in misery.

## 10:03:03

Boys stare out the panes,
say, "It's going to rain," and
taps confirm their words.

## 10:03:04

I've always loved how
thunder echoes into the
canyon, a wonder.

## 10:03:05

Looks like it will be
play inside for the remainder
of the morning.

## 10:03:06

Good thing it's almost
time for lunch; I'm about all
worded out today.

## 10:08:12

They put together
LEGOs for a while and are
perfectly content.

## 10:13:43

They play dress up, for
want of something better to
do; the rain patters.

## 10:13:45

Toes scrunched up, he tries
to fit into the shoes of
giants in his life.

## 10:17:34

They build block houses
for their cards—fight some, but mostly
collaborate.

## 10:25:57

Thumps, bumps, crashes—all
the sounds boys can make rattle
a house foundation.

## 10:26:14

Two falls in one morning
says he's tired, and today
will be a war.

## 10:27:43

They do puzzles and
it's the only respite I
get from wild action.

## 10:41:20

How many times must
I say the same things over
and over again?

## 10:41:23

How does one begin
to say what needs saying when
no one's listening?

## 10:53:10

In a moment of
silence I think—and sometimes
thinking's dangerous.

## 10:53:11

I can't stop the
worry today. It is a
runaway tornado.

## 10:53:12

It's the familiar
worries—am I enough, will
we make it through this?

## 10:53:13

But something else presses
at the edges, steals my
breath, panic clawing.

## 10:53:14

The invasives are
especially invasive
today. Won't let go.

## 10:53:15

Round and round they turn
like a tightening spiral
squeezing me breathless.

## 10:53:16

*Breathe,* I tell myself,
breathe, keeping breathing, in, out, for
all the good it does.

## 10:53:17

I can't breathe, I'm dying,
I look at my kids, I'm
dying. I'm dying.

## 10:53:18

So tight I can't breathe
or feel, I try to fling the
spiral far away.

## 10:53:19

The pain is always
worse the more numb I get before
it slices through.

## 10:53:20

Searing cold, then blasting
heat climbs up my arm, and
surely I am dead.

## 10:53:21

*Mama, are you okay?*
My vision clears, the black
spots recede, he's here.

## 10:53:22

*Yes, baby,* I say.
He's too young to know about
anxiety wars.

## 10:53:25

One is reading in
the corner; the two others
watch my every move.

## 10:53:27

I return to the
moment, see them, feel myself
stretch into lean lines.

## 10:53:30

One of them offers
to read a story to me;
I'll gladly listen.

## 10:53: 34

When he doesn't know
the words he makes up his own—
a book of nonsense.

## 10:54:06
We don't know all we
can about another's life—
that's why it looks good.

## 10:54:07
Some are anxious, some
depressed; maybe we're all just
a little broken.

11:00 AM

**11:01:42**

The house is a wreck,
but kids played together—that's
enough for today.

**11:02:34**

Or maybe enough
for this moment—the next one
they start their fighting.

**11:07:34**

Fight, fight, fight, fight, fight
all they seem to do is fight;
wish they'd be quiet.

**11:07:35**

The one who isn't
fighting stretches out next to
me, looking so cute.

**11:07:36**

He draws pictures while
I write stories—brilliance in
the making right here.

**11:07:37**

Why can't they be kind?
Why must they endlessly fight
about silly things?

**11:13:27**

Some days I'm much more
tolerant of crying than
others. Today? Nope.

**11:13:28**

So it's now time for
lunch, even though it's thirty
minutes too early.

**11:13:29**

They must be protected
from my wrath; they don't want
to see explosions.

**11:13:32**

Slap sandwiches
together, cut carrots, throw in
some red grapes: Lunch time!

## 11:13:48

The quietest moments
in my house are when boys
stuff food in faces.

## 11:41:49

I wanted to read
today, but someone in my
house kept on talking.

## 11:41:50

*Interruptions,* I
say, *are not polite. You can't
hear the story well.*

## 11:41:51

He keeps talking, wants
to finish what he's saying.
One book takes hours.

## 11:41:52

(Not really. It takes a
a few extra minutes to
answer his questions.)

## 11:41:53
(It's just that I'm more
than ready for nap time. It's
been a long, wet day.)

## 11:42:20
They never want the
reading to end, because they
know stories are gifts.

## 11:43:12
I give them some silent
reading time so I can
pull out a book, too.

## 11:45:17
Instead of reading,
they play in their beds —so surprise!
Reading time's done.

## 11:45:18
*It's time for naps!* I
say, and they'll find a million
distractions toward beds.

## 11:45:23

Twins are the hardest
parenting challenge I've
encountered—doubly so.

## 11:45:25

It's not that they mean
to be—it's just that there are
two of them, always.

## 11:45:26

But the challenging
parts of life are what make us
who we are—stronger.

## 11:45:27

(At least I tell myself
this in order to live—
survival tactics.)

## 11:52:41

Silence is blissful;
I did not value it enough
before children.

## 11:52:45
All I need is a
little time to read and the
day's back in order.

## 11:59:58
Now it's time to get
to work, exercising my
imagination.

## 11:59:59
If we want to do
what's impossible, we first
attempt the absurd.

12:00 PM

**12:01:01**

Thunderstorms provide
the best backdrop to reading
and writing stories.

**12:02:58**

First I write fiction,
the most demanding task for
my brain to create.

**12:02:59**

Casting a vision's
about seeing what's
invisible to others.

**12:03:01**

I see what's invisible
and try to make it
visible to you.

**12:03:02**

Sometimes I do that
well; sometimes I fail miserably.
This is life.

## 12:03:03

Not just for a writer—
for everyone. We're all
learning how to dream.

## 12:03:05

Doubts always sneak in—
this is natural. I don't
listen to their lies.

## 12:03:06

It takes practice to
ignore the voices that tell
us who we can be.

## 12:03:07

You can be what you
always wanted to be: work,
practice, and become.

## 12:03:08

If you can't believe
in yourself, in your value
then, tell me, who can?

## 12:03:09

Hard work goes a long
way. My great-grandpa told me
that. I believed him.

## 12:03:10

So every moment my
children sleep, I arrange my
words on a page. Work.

## 12:03:11

The spaces are bigger
than you might think when you've
taken them captive.

## 12:31:37

Clanks sound from the
kitchen as he prepares our lunch.
I'm grateful for breaks.

## 12:43:18

Sometimes I'd like to
take a quick nap—until I
recall the last one.

## 12:43:19
(Opportunistic
children and naps don't mesh well,
if you're wondering.)

## 12:43:20
Returning to the
story invigorates me,
no longer tired.

## 12:43:21
I ponder many
things on the page, my best
thinking space—deep things like:

## 12:43:22
There are two sides to
me—one that is gently kind,
one that's a monster.

## 12:43:23
The appearance of
someone doesn't tell us much—
what's inside's worth more.

## 12:43:24

There is so much to
learn in the world if we live
in an earnest way.

## 12:43:25

And what does it mean
to live in an earnest way?
Be ourselves? Chase dreams?

## 12:43:56

Who are we, really,
when the masks are stripped away?
Are we so different?

## 12:59:59

The timer clangs; it's
time to move on to the next
line on the to-do.

1:00 PM

**1:01:01**

Essays, memoirs—I
love telling real-life stories
as much as fiction.

**1:01:02**

Some might say memoir
is just a glorified look
back, but it's vital.

**1:01:03**

If we do not look
back, tell me, how will we know
how to move forward?

**1:01:04**

I write about many
things—anxiety,
children, my family…

**1:01:05**

But mostly I write
about honesty, courage,
being who we are.

## 1:01:06

My thoughts fire at
random; I capture as much
as I can in words.

## 1:01:07

I work out my feelings:
take stock of my heart and
write myself to joy.

## 1:02:35

He wants it all—that's
what we fight about most; life's
made up of choices.

## 1:02:36

But the story of
my marriage is something
revolutionary:

## 1:02:37

We are partners in
all walks of our life: work, home,
play—and the dreaming.

**1:02:38**

When you wait for what's
best, you will be surprised how
good it really is.

**1:22:19**

Exhaustion is hard
to escape; my kids wear me
down day after day.

**1:22:20**

The hardest part is
shaping their hearts to be strong,
resilient, bold.

**1:22:21**

I give instruction,
they ask why—a hundred, a
thousand times a day.

**1:22:22**

But I don't want to
discourage that; I want to
embrace it fully.

## 1:22:23

Questions, after all,
are a window to change: we
question, we learn more.

## 1:22:24

Questions can, too, be
annoyances for a
parent: a paradox.

## 1:39:56

I take a quick break;
something is pressing at the
edges of my mind.

## 1:39:57

It's my old friend
anxiety. I shove him far
away; he'll be back.

## 1:39:58

My anxiety
sometimes gets so bad I see
what's not really there.

**1:39:59**

But anxiety
in my writing space is a
pest and nothing more.

**1:40:00**

The rain drums on the
windows. Thunder rumbles in
the distant canyon.

**1:40:01**

All I really want
to do on a rain day is
curl up with a book.

**1:40:02**

The rain continues
its rhythm on my pane; I
try on more topics.

**1:40:03**

Philosophy,
identity, these rich spaces
where I learn to breathe.

## 1:40:04

Even in the
deepest of winter I have with
me endless summer.

## 1:45:32

Many talk as if
they know all there is to know.
They're hot air balloons.

## 1:47:13

What is the measure
of a life between sunset
and sunrise? Moments.

## 1:48:49

What it takes to live
differently than all the rest:
courage and genius.

## 1:48:52

An ending place is
not always what it seems. At
times it's a new start.

## 1:49:01
What do we know of
pleasure if we cannot learn
to laugh at ourselves?

## 1:49:22
Reputation is
not as important as
living with great courage.

## 1:49:37
Who knew an old home
could hold the essence of who
you've been, who you'll be?

## 1:49:58
All the world in me,
but the question remains still:
Who will I become?

## 1:49:59
We know who we are,
but do we ever truly
know who we'll become?

## 1:59:54

I don't usually
think about what others will
think of my writing.

## 1:59:55

But when it's personal,
the thought always crosses
my mind: is this good?

## 1:59:56

What's the point of you
writing if you don't annoy
somebody somewhere?

## 1:59:57

What is the price of
silence? The benefits? How
do you weigh the two?

## 1:59:58

Why do we try so
hard to mask our weaknesses
when they are real strength?

## 1:59:59

I would like to be
brave on the page, so I share
my imperfections.

2:00 PM

**2:00:01**

When I can't think, when
writing feels too hard, I pick
up a different pen.

**2:00:02**

Poetry is where
I move next; sometimes stories
are easier there.

**2:00:03**

(So I want to do
more than just the one thing. Who
says I can't do it?)

**2:00:04**

I transport myself
back to the memories that
wait to be written.

**2:00:05**

Those from earlier
today, when my life revolved
around kids and love.

## 2:04:27

They huddled under
blankets, a book open as
they read in earnest.

## 2:04:28

Everything they touch
is an opportunity
for great destruction.

## 2:04:31

They colored themselves
green and thought no one would notice:
that's kid logic.

## 2:12:46

The laundry thumped while
banana bread scented rooms:
domesticity.

## 2:38:12

The poems fly off
my pen, hardly slowing down;
my hand is cramping.

## 2:38:13

Still I write, because
one never knows what sort of
treasure you'll find here.

## 2:40:57

The man of sorrows
finds easy expression but
difficult telling.

## 2:49:11

When a heart finds love
it's found a missing piece of
a wandering soul.

## 2:52:38

Listen to the song
I sing and you will hear the
secrets of my heart.

## 2:52:39

I wish a wish and
dream a dream and yet life is
so, so much better.

## 2:52:40

This is what poetry
has to tell me: that life
is worth the living.

## 2:52:41

Some days the whole world
feels like it's upside down, but
tomorrow's brand new.

## 2:52:42

It's an endless sort
of hope that echoes in all
our deepest spaces.

## 2:59:50

Ben comes in while I'm
finishing up, a little
earlier than planned.

## 2:59:51

It's not usually
a problem; we know how to
respect our work time.

## 2:59:52

We sit in stillness,
peacefully working, sharing
in a dream come true.

## 2:59:53

The problem is that
he's on the phone, and my music
doesn't hide it.

## 2:59:54

The hum of voices
is distracting today—I
cannot write a thing.

## 2:59:55

I'm done, two seconds
earlier than I'd planned to
be done—because voices.

## 2:59:56

I put down my pen
with a dirty look at the
insensitive man.

## 2:59:57
(I'll forgive him later;
this is one of our many
dances through love.)

## 2:59:58
He shrugs in apology;
already I'm over
it. No big deal.

## 2:59:59
It's time to head down
the stairs; boys will be home soon
and madness ensues.

3:00 PM

**3:02:45**

I have a few blissful
moments alone, before
the door crashes wide.

**3:07:12**

I spend them in
preparation: loading dishes,
wiping counters clean.

**3:10:04**

Then I wait by the
door, listening for their
familiar laughter, words.

**3:12:38**

Slam through the door, sling
backpacks down, unload lunch stuff:
the after-school rush.

**3:12:39**

It's two minutes in;
the requests and word counts soar:
two hundred million.

## 3:12:40
All at the same time—
that's what makes it stressful
and so overwhelming.

## 3:12:41
The loudest moments
are sometimes the hardest to
control and enjoy.

## 3:12:42
One talks more than the
rest, because this is his mode
of being: to talk.

## 3:12:43
When he's learning
something new, he can't stop talking—
which is near always.

## 3:12:44
I love to hear him
talk, truly I do; there is
just so much to do.

## 3:12:45
He follows me around,
never missing a single
beat—unlike me.

## 3:12:46
They are all back home
and the world is speeding by
all over again.

## 3:20:00
Now it's time for them
to sit and read: something they
do with great pleasure.

## 3:20:21
They read together
on the couch, silently still,
linked at the shoulders.

## 3:21:14
When they're quiet, I
sit down, too. Might as well get
some reading time in.

## 3:24:57

Is there anything
so lovely as uncovering
knowledge and truth?

## 3:32:11

He sits beside me
reading the same book he's read
three times already.

## 3:51:00

Story draws me in;
when the timer clangs, I want
to finish this page.

## 3:51:01

Reading is quite
challenging when you have six clowns
begging attention.

## 3:52:08

He hums wherever
he goes, reading a book,
eating dinner, sleeping.

## 3:52:09

He sits down at the
piano to compose what's
singing in his head.

## 3:52:34

The piano's notes
have fallen flat but are lifted
by their played joy.

## 3:54:03

The clouds hang low in
a gray curtain—no sun, and
finally, no heat.

## 3:54:04

I tell them to go
outside and play; it's no longer
too hot to run.

## 3:54:05

And if they stay in
here one more minute, my brain
is gonna explode.

## 3:58:23

There is a cloud
following me wherever I
go, raining on me.

## 3:58:24

I should be happy,
right? I have a good life—kids,
husband, health, and love.

## 3:58:25

But sometimes the cloud
is unexplainable;
sometimes it is just there.

## 3:58:26

I notice it but
try not to pay attention
to it; walk with it.

## 3:58:27

I know the tides will
rise and fall and I will feel
better in short time.

## 3:58:28

Or long time, maybe.
It doesn't matter. The point:
it'll get better.

## 3:58:29

I know this, so I
can let myself feel the cloud,
let myself feel down.

## 3:59:59

I find love notes all
over the house—this is being
the mom of boys.

4:00 PM

**4:00:00**

Technology time
is the bane of my existence.
Hate it. Need it.

**4:01:27**

He tells me why he
needs more tech time: I try
to listen to him.

**4:01:28**

I watch him give a
presentation with such passion,
like a genius.

**4:03:29**

I compliment him
on his presentation—the
answer is still no.

**4:33:30**

He fights me on it
for half an hour. I flee
to my room for rest.

## 4:34:51

I am alone in
my room; the house is quiet:
what are they doing?

## 4:34:53

They are fighting,
arguing over who had something
first: I don't know.

## 4:34:54

The boys argue like
this is how they talk. It grows
old, stale, and ugly.

## 4:34:55

Someone gave us a
punching bag—now brothers don't
pummel each other.

## 4:35:22

Music spills from the
top floor, another song is
written. Hope today.

## 4:35:23

We all stop, listen,
breathe, and try to remember
that thing we call love.

## 4:38:19

Then the songwriter
clomps down the stairs to see what
his family's doing.

## 4:38:20

*Someone's coming by*,
my husband tells me. Oh. I
was not quite prepared.

## 4:38:21

I like to be prepared;
there are standards when you
invite visitors.

## 4:38:22

*Didn't I tell you?*
he says. *No*, I say. *Could have
sworn I did*, he says.

## 4:38:23

So I'm a little
annoyed; I'll have to pick up
the house, wash dishes.

## 4:38:24

But there's no time—the
doorbell rings and all I pick
up are some papers.

## 4:38:25

(The boys have trashed this
house, and it'll be so
embarrassing to show.)

## 4:38:26

But I open the
door anyway; a smile
greets me, some old friends.

## 4:38:27

We talk for a while
and never once do they mention
my awful house.

## 4:45:16
(Maybe I put too
much pressure on myself, then.
People don't notice.)

## 4:45:17
An unexpected
meeting happened today—but
I survived surprise.

## 4:45:18
Now they've gone; what have
my boys done in this time of
such split attention?

## 4:45:58
*Will you come play with
us?* they ask. I have a few
more minutes to spare.

## 4:45:59
The clouds hover in
sheets above us, sliced off as
if carefully hung.

## 4:46:15

They harvest flowers
from the field, I try to tuck
them behind my ear.

## 4:46:16

Here's a flower for
you, pink around the edges.
Put it in your hair.

## 4:47:34

Playing catch with a
car, back and forth, just to see
his beautiful smile.

## 4:48:57

An airplane thunders
overhead, but we can't see
it for the thick clouds.

## 4:48:58

We make up stories
about where the plane is headed,
who's on it, why.

**4:48:59**

Imagination
is cultivated in these
little playful games.

**4:49:59**

They're swinging sky-high,
I'm trying to write a good
poem. They're winning.

**4:50:00**

It's time to start dinner;
they'll play outside while I
cook—the only way.

**4:50:01**

Except the youngest
one, who follows me inside
and entertains me.

**4:51:02**

He is walking his
little wooden dog as if
it's alive. Precious.

## 4:53:23
He's sitting on the
floor, reading a book, even
though he cannot read.

## 4:54:46
Those eyes, looking for
me everywhere; he finds a
safe, warm home in me.

## 4:55:14
Cooking is a time
for deep wonderings. I let
them float through my mind.

## 4:55:15
My wonderings are
random, circling family,
friends, hopes, and big dreams.

## 4:55:16
I don't know that a
single syllable out of
his mouth was the truth.

## 4:55:17

If I could only
believe in myself…just think
of what I could do.

## 4:55:18

Life is dangerous
enough without our need to
wage unending wars.

## 4:59:22

I look out the window:
they are still jumping, still
laughing, still playing.

## 4:59:23

Jumping, all day they
are jumping and they never
once grow weary. How?

## 4:59:24

It's a wondrous thing
to be a child; too bad we
don't realize it then.

**5:01:03**

Puttering around
the kitchen, I cook the meal
they'll complain about.


**5:03:29**

He wants to play, I
must cook—but how much longer
will he ask me this?


**5:03:30**

They'll complain about
it and then they'll ask for seconds—
paradoxes.


**5:29:17**

It's finally done;
the youngest helps me set the
table with bowls, spoons.


**5:29:46**

I yell outside: *It's
time for dinner*, but they pretend
they don't hear me.

## 5:29:47

They ask for snacks a
billion times a day but don't
come in for dinner.

## 5:30:01

As soon as their daddy
comes down, they race inside.
*Soup again?* they say.

## 5:30:02

(I don't tell them it's
my favorite thing to cook:
undemanding, easy.)

## 5:30:03

The smell of boy is
so putrid my eyes water,
and my nose curls tight.

## 5:30:31

We link hands and pray—
this is the beginning of
every great dinner.

## 5:30:35

And then we settle
in for the loud, lively,
engaging discussion.

## 5:30:57

The dinnertime
discussions are my favorite things:
necessary, thrilling.

## 5:30:58

We get to know who
our children are, see glimpses
of who they'll become.

## 5:30:59

All while they suck dry
the soup they claimed they didn't
like; now it's tasty.

## 5:31:00

Maybe it's the
discussion that seasons it—or
just my cooking skill.

## 5:31:01
(It's definitely
not the cooking; I have
never been a great cook.)

## 5:31:02
I know they are
getting what they need from us
around a full table.

## 5:31:03
If we want a new
world, we have to learn how to
ask the right questions.

## 5:31:04
We try to ask those
questions of our children: who
do you want to be?

## 5:35:21
What would you change about
the world around you? What
hopes live in your heart?

## 5:42:45

What do you find yourself
thinking about the most?
How could dreams come true?

## 5:42:46

What does this look like
at the dinner table? It
looks like wild madness.

## 5:42:47

But we know it's
important to power through; they
need this time with us.

## 5:43:59

We talk about hard
things—sickness in the family,
injustice, bullies.

## 5:45:28

What's happening in
the world, our frustrations, our
fears. Love, joy, and hope.

## 5:47:29

What can we say of
hope? It is unshakeable,
brave, fluttering still.

## 5:58:34

At times Ben and I
talk to each other, but kids
aren't great at quiet.

## 5:58:35

We're trying to have
a conversation and there
are too many kids.

## 5:58:36

And our annoyance
soars: can we just finish our
sentence now, please? Please?

## 5:58:37

(It's better to talk
in the privacy of your
room; kid noise is loud.)

**5:58:38**

(One day they won't be
here to interrupt—and we'll
likely miss it then.)

**5:59:27**

(So we set our
annoyance aside and return
to their silly talk.)

**5:59:28**

(Kids can only be
serious for so long, and
we've used up their store.)

**5:59:41**

So we smile and
enjoy the silliness. This,
too, is important.

6:00 PM

**6:15:29**

Yogurt with cacao
nibs and frozen blueberries
is the best dessert.

**6:18:31**

*I love this song*, he
says, wiggling in his seat and
singing his heart out.

**6:18:32**

It looks so fun we
decide to have an impromptu
dance session: win.

**6:21:57**

It's time for chores now,
and nobody wants to be
the one who must sweep.

**6:21:58**

Cleanup time is not
their favorite time; but it
builds their character.

## 6:21:59

There is one who must
be reminded of our
ritual every day.

## 6:22:00

We've been doing the
drill for thousands of days now—
but he still forgets.

## 6:22:01

He is always ready
to reach for a book, to
hear a good story.

## 6:22:02

But the family is
a team, and we need everyone
working on chores.

## 6:25:46

The dishwasher churns
and spins; kids shriek outside and
somewhere a heart warms.

## 6:25:51

He holds onto me
like only I can carry
him up the mountain.

## 6:25:52

I'm beginning to
feel spent, overwhelmed, anxious
in my parenting.

## 6:25:53

Too much togetherness
is difficult for an
introverted mom.

## 6:25:54

I try not to be
too hard on myself; doesn't
mean I don't love them.

## 6:25:55

Children have all the
nonsense they could need to
navigate the world well.

## 6:25:56

I think we'll start baths
a little early tonight—
for their good and mine.

## 6:25:57

Instead, their daddy
suggests a dip in the
neighborhood pool. Good plan.

## 6:25:58

I bow out, though, say
I could do some cleaning up—
it is mostly true.

## 6:25:59

*Why don't you go with
us?* my second son says. I
can't explain it now.

## 6:26:00

He's too young to
understand the pressure on
women to look perfect.

## 6:32:13
They go to the pool,
while I stay home with my
ruined body hidden.

## 6:32:14
What could you do if
you broke the ropes binding you
and roamed the world free?

## 6:32:15
I have never once
been comfortable in my
own physical skin.

## 6:32:16
I have always wanted
a better one—thinner,
smoother, more perfect.

## 6:32:17
Every year it keeps
me from enjoying the pool
with my swimming boys.

## 6:32:18

I tried a year of
body love—and I made it
three tormented months

## 6:32:19

before I had to
stop looking at myself in
the mirror at all.

## 6:32:20

Sometimes it's easier
to ignore it than study
it with pleasure.

## 6:32:21

Maybe I didn't
try hard enough. Maybe I'll
give it one more try.

## 6:52:49

Tonight, while they're at
the pool, I clean, pick up toys,
wait for their return.

## 6:52:50
I think—about life,
about family, about
who I am inside.

7:00

PM

## 7:03:34

I'm waiting outside
when they come screeching into
the front yard, soaking.

## 7:03:35

*Go run around*, he
tells them. *Dry off a little.*
Leave parents to talk.

## 7:03:36

We stare toward the
west, sky aflame, hands touching,
kids stalking the yard.

## 7:08:52

His voice is louder
than mine, so he calls them to
the door. Time to read.

## 7:09:11

A library is
a world of knowledge in the
collection of books.

## 7:09:12

And we've created
one in our home, where we read,
write, and imagine.

## 7:10:01

They're not as quiet
in this library as our
local one—it's home.

## 7:10:02

It's manageable
until they start fighting over
the same novel.

## 7:10:03

I could enjoy the
six of them together if
they'd just stop fighting.

## 7:10:04

(I know I should enjoy
the six of them regardless;
some days are hard.)

## 7:13:48

A story begs their
attention and they're quiet
again: This is peace.

## 7:14:39

They climb all over
him while he's reading them their
go-to-bed stories.

## 7:27:13

They all love reading
and this is one of the great
pleasures in my life.

## 7:38:22

Kisses, hugs, courage,
we send them to bed with
everything they could need.

## 7:38:23

The older ones get
to stay up a few minutes
later—if they read.

## 7:40:28

Wisps of cloud glow pink
in the evening sky; a golden
sun, breathtaking.

## 7:41:50

They sit around the
love seat writing stories they'll
read aloud later.

## 7:41:51

(They don't like to sit
in the love seat—it shoves them
too near each other.)

## 7:41:52

They're subdued tonight,
so I keep waiting for the
bomb to fall—will it?

## 7:45:06

Time for bed, and they
go right down—there's something strange
in the air tonight.

## 7:45:42

If your life were a
song, what would be the chorus?
The verse? The tempo?

## 7:45:43

Mine has quiet sounds
tonight—kids whispering, fans
blowing, life breathing.

## 7:45:44

Pages shift against
a toilet paper roll, a
fan blazing behind.

## 7:46:01

It can't be that easy.
It's never been that easy.
He looks at me.

## 7:46:02

What do you want to
do? I don't know, what do you
want to do? Don't know.

## 7:49:32

We decide on a
movie, some unhealthy snacks,
a little talk time.

## 7:52:09

As soon as the movie
starts, they burst into our
room to see it, too.

## 7:52:10

I roll my eyes, he
puts them all back to bed—*and
this time stay there*. (Please.)

## 7:58:14

(They don't. As soon as
they know we're doing something,
they need everything.)

## 7:58:38

We try to have a
date in our bedroom, and they
don't leave us alone.

## 7:59:03

Utopia is
very hard to imagine
on a given day.

8:00 PM

## 8:01:01

Their sounds still reach me
in the confines of my room;
we need to sound proof.

## 8:03:23

The door opens. He
is there, grinning, proud, silly.
*Time for bed*, I say.

## 8:03:24

He just wants one more
kiss and then he'll go to bed
and stay, he tells me.

## 8:05:19

It's time for bed, but
they are wired, making noise,
avoiding bedtime.

## 8:05:20

My husband goes out
to tell them to sleep; maybe
this time they'll listen.

## 8:05:21

Someone, though, starts
arguing; I know exactly
which child it is.

## 8:05:22

Parenting a strong-
willed child is a constant
clash of titan strength.

## 8:05:23

I am glad he is
strong-willed; it will serve him well.
But a pain for me.

## 8:05:24

At least the me who
would like nothing more than to
relax this evening.

## 8:05:25

I take out a journal
and write—this has always
been how I center.

## 8:05:26

In the small spaces
I jot down my memories,
careful to keep them.

## 8:05:27

Thoughts creep in while my
husband is gone; I can't always
stop their creeping.

## 8:05:28

The headache has become
a living, breathing thing,
alive and vicious.

## 8:05:29

Sometimes I need a
good, long break from all the male
people in my house.

## 8:05:30

I am okay. I
am okay. If I say it
enough, it is true.

## 8:05:31

My body feels weary,
like it's been flattened
under a semi truck.

## 8:05:32

I was supposed to
rest today—but of course that
didn't quite happen.

## 8:05:33

(How does a mother
ever truly rest? It's a
necessary dream.)

## 8:05:34

(I just didn't
execute it well. I worked while
they played. That's no fun.)

## 8:05:35

Play is our rest; we
need more time to play if we
expect to be great.

## 8:05:36

Play comes in many
forms; we have to find the right
kind of play for us.

## 8:05:37

When I'm feeling
overwhelmed, all I need's a
quiet place and a book.

## 8:05:38

So I know reading
is a form of play for me—
I relax and breathe.

## 8:09:57

I rouse myself, though—
we have a date in our room
and kids are in bed.

## 8:09:58

There's something special
about the time when all the
kids have gone to sleep.

## 8:09:59

A parent must take
advantage of kids sleeping;
we turn on a show.

## 8:11:12

A fan hums in the
background while I wait for him
to bring me cheese dip.

## 8:26:41

I notice I don't
look at him enough anymore.
Tonight I do.

## 8:26:42

It's an overwhelming
life, but the best way through
it is holding hands.

## 8:58:47

We shut down our date
and turn in early because
bedtime comes swiftly.

## 8:58:48

Light sweeps out like the
wings of a firefly—a
romantic shading.

## 8:58:49

Conversation in
the late-night house strips away
our inhibition.

## 8:58:50

His voice is a low
rumble, vibrating through my
head, comforting me.

## 8:58:51

He's my lover, my
friend; he gives me shade and opens
my heart's flower.

## 8:59:56

When his breathing evens
beside me, the thoughts
begin to come alive.

## 8:59:57

I wonder if I
spend enough time with my children,
if I know them.

## 8:59:58

I wonder if I
have been enough for them, for
him, for the whole world.

## 8:59:59

Each day must be judged
by the seeds we plant, not by
the harvest we sow.

9:00 PM

**9:00:00**

Once the wondering
door is open, it takes force
to close it again.

**9:00:01**

The hum of a fan
drowns out everything but the
loud thoughts in my head.

**9:00:02**

I try to sleep, but
thoughts crowd in, begging me to
worry, solve, create.

**9:00:03**

The worries line up
like sentinels watching from
a constant shadow.

**9:00:04**

When the hour is
late, I find myself thinking
of dangerous things.

## 9:00:05
I know the hour
isn't exactly late—but
this is late for me.

## 9:00:07
What if there is something
more to this catch in my
throat? What if it's bad?

## 9:00:08
What if those allergies
are not just allergies?
What if it is worse?

## 9:00:09
What if the doctors
aren't able to cure my
brother? What if he dies?

## 9:00:10
What if something happens
to our car? How will we
run all the errands?

## 9:00:11
How will we work? How will we recover from a setback like that one?

## 9:00:12
What if I never publish another book? What if I can't keep up?

## 9:00:13
What if one of my children is lost, hurt, damaged, bullied, broken, killed?

## 9:00:14
It only takes a few seconds to run through all the scenarios.

## 9:02:57
Anxiety runs cold, hot, numb, excruciating—and always there.

**9:03:36**

I turn my thoughts to
happier things; it's like turning
a ship around.

**9:03:59**

I think about love—
the beauty of loving
another and the world.

**9:04:00**

What is love but
seeing a miracle
invisible to others?

**9:04:01**

Love is courage and
courage is love—the most
dangerous form of each.

**9:04:02**

The two ingredients
for a happy life: love
and constant laughter.

## 9:05:45

Sleep comes softly, on
a silent breath, a gentle
murmur into bliss.

## 9:05:46

Where do the days go?
Like the birds, they fly away
to a distant end.

THE

END

## About the Author

Rachel is the author of two poetry books, *This is How You Know* and *Life: a definition of terms*, and a middle grade novel-in-verse, *The Colors of the Rain*. She has been writing poetry since the time she could hold a pencil and make what passed as letters on the page. Her first introduction into poetry was the brilliance of Shel Silverstein, whom she still reads today. She recently introduced her sons to the hilarious Jack Prelutsky poem, "Homework! Oh Homework!" which was one of her favorites as a kid. They loved it (as she still does).

Her poems for children and adults can be read in literary magazines and online publications around the world.

Rachel lives with her husband and six boys in San Antonio, Texas. She daily reads poetry (as well as many, many books) to her children, because poetry, she says, contains the essence of life, and reading, she says, is the gateway to a future of promise.

## Author's Note

My dear reader,

It is so easy, in the minutiae of a day, to lose our sense of self and who we are. It is easy to come so close to the end of ourselves that we cannot help but say, "Is this really all there is?" And when we are caught up in the discontent or the frustration of a moment, it is easy to believe that this *is* really all there is.

But it is not all there is. We have only to still ourselves and sink into a moment—listening to, watching, tasting it—to know that a moment is so much more than what appears on the surface.

I hope *The Book of Uncommon Hours* has given you a glimpse into what life might be like if we take it one moment, one hour, one revelation at a time.

If you have enjoyed this book, one very simple thing you can do to get it into other hands is to leave a review wherever you bought it. Reviews help increase a book's visibility and ensure that new readers find it.

You can also tell a friend about it—because a writer's best friend (besides her husband, sister, and mother; I'm speaking about this writer, not all) is a word-of-mouth recommendation.

Thank you for your support and for reading all the way to the author's note.

You are treasured, revered, and so very loved.

In love,
Rachel

## Acknowledgments

This book was made possible by:

My husband, who both provided material for the poems and also ensured that kids did not interrupt when I mumbled, "I need to write something down real quick." You are a partner in every sense of the word, and I am so glad I get to be your wife and bask in your love.

My children, who fill my days with so much inspiration I hardly know what to do with it all. You have written so many books for me (metaphorically speaking).

Emily Brontë, whose collections of poetry I read during the entire writing of this book.

You. If you've made it this far, you are a true believer in my work. I am humbled, honored, and grateful. Thank you for your trust.

# Enjoy more poetry from Rachel Toalson

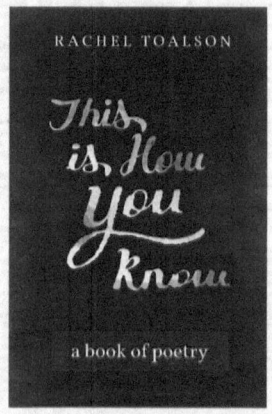
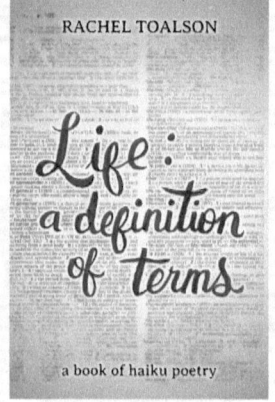

racheltoalson.com/poetry

Rachel Toalson Poetry
# Starter Library

**Enjoy more of Rachel Toalson's poetry with these free downloads.**

*To get your FREE books, visit ***
*RachelToalson.com/FreeBook*

*Must be 13 or older to be eligible

www.ingramcontent.com/pod-product-compliance
Lightning Source LLC
Chambersburg PA
CBHW021437080526
44588CB00009B/565